EASY DESSERT RECIPES
FOR EVERY OCCASION

ALEX RAY

summersdale

PUDS

Summersdale Publishers Ltd
46 West Street
Chichester
West Sussex
PO19 1RP
UK

www.summersdale.com

Printed and bound in Malta

ISBN: 978-1-84953-814-5

Substantial discounts on bulk quantities of Summersdale books are available to corporations, professional associations and other organisations. For details contact Nicky Douglas by telephone: +44 (0) 1243 756902, fax: +44 (0) 1243 786300 or email: nicky@summersdale.com.

CONTENTS

Retro puddings...67

Dinner-party puddings...............................81

"

FOR WHEN YOU FANCY
SOMETHING SWEET, BUT
DON'T HAVE TIME TO
SPEND HOURS IN THE
KITCHEN, THESE RECIPES
ARE PROOF THAT A FAST
FIX CAN BE EVERY BIT
AS GOOD AS A COMPLEX
CULINARY CREATION.

"

EASY
PUDDINGS

BAKED APPLES

Nothing says autumn like a plump baked apple bursting from its skin and oozing with fruit and honey. Simple is good!

Ingredients (per person)

1 cooking apple
2 tsp dried fruit (sultanas, raisins, currants)
1 tsp honey

Preparation method

Preheat the oven to 200°C.

Wash and core the apple and place on a piece of foil that will easily wrap around the apple.

Combine honey with dried fruit then fill the cavity in the apple.

Wrap the apple with the foil and bake for 45 minutes.

Remove from oven, remove foil, allow to cool slightly, and serve with natural yogurt or cream.

AVOCADO CHOCOLATE MOUSSE

Quick and easy, plus you get brownie points for eating one of your five a day for pud. See whether your fellow diners can guess the magic ingredient.

———————— *Serves 4* ————————

Ingredients

2 ripe avocados
1 tbsp unsweetened cocoa powder
1 tbsp honey
1 tbsp cold water

Preparation method

Split the avocados and take out the pips, then spoon out the flesh into a bowl.

Add the cocoa, honey and water and blitz with a hand blender until smooth.

Divide between individual glasses and chill until you're ready to serve.

MICROWAVE SPONGE IN A MUG

Pushed for time? Home alone? There are times when making a full-sized dessert just can't be justified. But does that mean you need to go without pud? Heavens no. The very thought…

———————————| Serves 2 |———————————

Ingredients

50 g butter or margarine (plus extra for greasing)

50 g golden caster sugar

1 medium egg

50 g self-raising flour

1–2 tbsp milk

2 tbsp golden syrup or raspberry jam

Preparation method

Cream the butter and sugar until fluffy. You can do this by hand or with an electric whisk.

Slowly mix in the egg and then fold in the flour until fully combined.

Add enough milk to form a dropping texture, i.e. it drops slowly from a spoon rather than stays welded to it when you hold it up.

Take two microwave-safe mugs and put a spoon of jam or syrup in the bottom of each, then top with half of the sponge mixture each.

Microwave on high for 3 minutes or until firm to the touch.

> ### Tip
>
> This one-egg mixture makes two mug cakes. But you don't have to share!
>
> Make sure you use mugs that are safe for the microwave and are large enough to allow the cake to rise. Remember, the syrup or jam will be very, very hot.

SALTED CARAMEL SAUCE

More topping than dessert, it's true – but it's also the fastest way to turn boring shop-bought ice cream into a dreamy, creamy pudding. Also livens up a baked apple no end.

―――――――――――――――――――― ⊢ *Serves 6–8* ⊢ ――――――――――――――――――――

Ingredients

100 g butter
200 g soft light brown sugar
125 ml double cream
1 tsp sea salt

Preparation method

Cut the butter into pieces and then place all the ingredients into a saucepan and stir over a low heat until the butter and sugar have melted.

Bring to a simmer and cook for a couple of minutes, stirring occasionally, until you have a rich, golden sauce.

Allow to cool slightly before serving over ice cream or with the dessert of your choice.

GRIDDLED PEACHES WITH AMARETTO CREAM

Peaches and almond are a perfect combination. This pud is proof that simple doesn't need to lack sophistication.

———————— Serves 4 ————————

Ingredients

150 ml double cream
1½ tbsp amaretto
1 tbsp icing sugar

4 amaretti biscuits
4 peaches

Preparation method

Whip the cream until it forms soft peaks. Gently fold in the amaretto and sugar. Refrigerate until needed.

Crumble the biscuits and set aside.

Halve and stone the peaches, then heat a griddle pan (or grill) and cook the fruit for 3 minutes on each side.

Serve immediately with the amaretto cream and the biscuit crumbs scattered on top.

YOGURT BRÛLÉE

The (much) easier, healthier cousin of the crème brûlée.
Not many desserts work perfectly for breakfast – but this
is the exception to the rule.

──────────────┤ *Serves 4* ├──────────────

Ingredients

150 g raspberries and/or strawberries
400 g natural yogurt
2 tbsp sugar (caster or muscovado)

Preparation method

Divide the fruit between 4 heatproof ramekins. If using
strawberries, hull and chop them first.

Top the fruit with the yogurt.

Sprinkle the sugar evenly across the surface of each pot.

If you have a blowtorch, use this to melt the sugar until
it caramelises and turns golden. Otherwise, put the pots
under a preheated grill to achieve the same effect – this

should take a couple of minutes, but watch carefully as it can burn easily.

Molten caramel is extremely hot, so leave the pots to cool for a few minutes before serving.

Tip

Fruit compote works really well in place of fresh fruit. Buy ready-made or lightly stew the fruit of your choice, draining excess juice and cooling before dividing between the pots.

KEY LIME PIE

There's hardly any actual cooking involved in this take on the American classic. Which probably makes it more of a lazy lime pie… though you'd never know from the taste.

———————— ┤ *Serves 8* ├ ————————

Ingredients

200 g digestive biscuits
100 g butter
5 limes
300 ml double cream
1 x 397-g can condensed milk
Whipped cream to serve

Preparation method

Preheat the oven to 150°C.

Crush the biscuits into fine crumbs.

Melt the butter and combine with the biscuit crumbs until thoroughly mixed.

Tip into a 22-cm loose-bottomed tart tin and press down firmly into the base and up the sides to form an even shell.

Bake for 8–10 minutes, remove from the oven and leave to cool fully.

Zest and juice the limes.

In a large bowl, mix together the cream and condensed milk – once combined, stir in the lime juice and three quarters of the zest. The mixture will thicken as soon as the juice is added.

Pour into the tart shell and chill until firm.

Before serving, top with whipped cream and decorate with the rest of the lime zest.

"

THE HEIGHT OF FASHION?
PERHAPS NOT. BUT THERE'S
A REASON THAT THESE
CLASSIC DESSERTS HAVE
NEVER DISAPPEARED FROM
THE MENU – BECAUSE
THEY'RE IRRESISTIBLE AND
UTTERLY DELICIOUS.

"

TRADITIONAL PUDDINGS

BREAD AND BUTTER PUDDING

Economical, easy and always a winner. Traditional? Yes.
A crowd-pleaser? Absolutely.

———————————————— ⊣ *Serves 4* ⊢ ————————————————

Ingredients

25 g butter

8 slices of white bread

50 sultanas

2 tsp ground cinnamon

2 eggs

25 g caster sugar

350 ml milk

60 ml double cream

1 tbsp demerara sugar

1 tsp freshly grated nutmeg

Preparation method

Grease a 1-litre ovenproof dish.

Spread butter on each slice of bread, cut off the crusts,
and cut into triangles.

Place a layer of the bread in the dish, topped with a layer
of sultanas and a sprinkling of cinnamon.

Repeat this layering process until you have used up all
the bread.

In a bowl, crack the eggs and add the caster sugar, then whisk until combined.

Gently warm the milk over a low heat and pour into the bowl. Add the cream and stir well to form a custard. Strain if necessary, to remove any curdled milk or cooked egg.

Pour the custard onto the bread pudding, and top with the demerara sugar and the nutmeg. Leave to stand for 30 minutes.

Preheat the oven to 180°C.

Place the dish in a roasting pan and fill the roasting pan halfway up with boiling water. Bake for 35 minutes, or until golden brown.

Tip

Bread that's a couple of days old works better than fresh. Slightly stale is fine! Also try using brioche, croissants or even hot cross buns in place of the bread – this is the perfect way to use up whatever you have floating around the kitchen!

STICKY TOFFEE PUDDING

One of the most popular puds in the land – and that surely comes as no surprise. Rich sponge and silky sauce combine to form the perfect partnership.

──────────────┤ Serves 4 ├──────────────

Ingredients

For the sponge:

225 g dates

300 ml tea (freshly made and still hot)

110 g butter

175 g demerara sugar

3 eggs (beaten)

225 g self-raising flour

1 tsp bicarbonate of soda

1 tsp vanilla extract

For the sauce:

110 g butter

175 g demerara sugar

110 g caster sugar

275 g golden syrup

225 ml double cream

1 tsp vanilla essence

Preparation method

Preheat the oven to 180°C. Grease an ovenproof dish and chop the dates (removing stones if necessary).

Pour the tea into a large bowl, then add the dates, and allow to cool for 15 minutes.

Beat the butter and sugar in a separate bowl, then gradually add the eggs.

Sift in the flour, bicarbonate of soda and vanilla extract. Stir until combined and smooth.

Pour in the date-and-tea mixture and combine.

Transfer the mixture to the dish, and bake for 60–90 minutes.

Meanwhile, heat the butter, demerara and caster sugar and the golden syrup in a small pan over a low heat, whisking continuously. Remove from the heat, and stir in the cream and vanilla essence. Return to the heat for a further 2–3 minutes until smooth.

Pour the sauce over the sponge and serve warm.

SPOTTED DICK

Leave memories of school dinners behind with just one mouthful of this version of the true British classic.

⊣ *Serves 6–8* ⊢

Ingredients

300 g plain flour
2 tsp baking powder
150 g shredded suet
75 g caster sugar
110 g currants
Grated zest of 1 lemon
200 ml milk
Butter for greasing

Preparation method

In a large bowl, sift the flour and add the baking powder, suet, sugar, currants and lemon zest, and mix well.

Gradually add the milk, stirring well to form a dough.

Grease a pudding basin with butter. Transfer the dough into the basin and cover with baking paper. Tie a piece of string around the edge to hold the paper in place, then place a damp tea towel on top and tie again to secure it in place.

Place the pudding basin in a large saucepan, filling two thirds with cold water. Cover, bring to the boil, and simmer for 1 hour, checking periodically to ensure it hasn't boiled dry.

SUSSEX POND PUDDING

When Sussex meets suet... the result is this intensely lemony delight.

———————————— ⊢ *Serves 6* ⊣ ————————————

Ingredients

For the pastry:

225 g self-raising flour
110 g shredded suet
90 ml milk
60 ml water

For the filling:

200 g butter
200 g light brown sugar
2 large lemons

Preparation method

Grease a 1½-litre pudding basin.

In a large bowl, sift the flour and mix in the suet.

Gradually pour in the milk and water together, stirring continuously to form a dough. Leave aside a quarter of the dough to be used later.

On a lightly-floured work surface, roll out the remaining dough to form a large round. Use this to line the pudding basin.

Dice the butter and put half, together with half the sugar, into the bottom of the pudding basin. Use a skewer to make several holes through the lemons (unpeeled). Place them in the pudding basin, then top up with the remaining butter and sugar.

Use the remaining pastry to form a round lid, pressing the edges together to seal. Place baking paper over the top of the basin, and then cover with aluminium foil. Use string to secure.

Boil the basin in a large, covered pan for 3–4 hours, topping up the water to come halfway up the basin throughout cooking.

TREACLE TART

Harry Potter's favourite pud. A slice of this will certainly bring magic to any mealtime.

Serves 6–8

Ingredients

For the pastry:

110 g butter
225 g plain flour
1 egg, beaten
1 tbsp cold water

For the filling:

450 g golden syrup
75 g fresh white breadcrumbs
Pinch of ground ginger (optional)
Grated zest of 1 lemon
Juice of ½ lemon

Preparation method

Dice the butter. Place in a large bowl, sift in the flour and rub together using your fingertips. Fold in the egg to form a dough, adding water if necessary.

On a lightly floured work surface, knead the dough until smooth.

Line a 23-cm tart tin with the dough, prick the base with a fork, and chill in the fridge for 30 minutes.

Preheat the oven to 190°C.

Line the pastry with baking paper, fill with ceramic baking beans, and blind bake for 15 minutes. If you don't have baking beans, you can use dried pulses or rice instead.

Remove the baking paper and beans, and return to the oven for a further 5 minutes, or until golden brown.

In a large bowl, combine the syrup, breadcrumbs, ginger, lemon zest and juice, then pour into the pastry case.

Bake for 30 minutes.

APPLE PIE

Great things stand the test of time and this is no exception. It's as sweet as… well, apple pie. Serve it with cream or vanilla ice cream or both!

———————————— ⊦ *Serves 6* ⊦ ————————————

Ingredients

For the pastry:

340 g plain flour

Pinch of salt

150 g butter

1 tbsp caster sugar

1 egg (beaten)

1 tsp of water

1 tbsp milk

For the filling:

700 g cooking apples

Juice of ½ lemon

110 g sultanas

75 g brown sugar

Grated zest of 1 orange

Pinch of ground cinnamon

Pinch of freshly grated
   nutmeg

1 tbsp caster sugar to serve

Preparation method

Preheat the oven to 200°C. In a large bowl, combine the flour, salt and butter, and rub together until it resembles breadcrumbs.

Add the sugar, egg and a splash of water to form a dough.

Knead on a lightly floured work surface, then roll out gently. Use two thirds of the pastry to line a 1-litre pie dish.

Peel, core and slice the apples and sprinkle with the lemon juice.

Layer the apples, sultanas, sugar, orange zest, cinnamon and nutmeg in the pie dish.

Use the remaining pastry to form the pie lid, brushing the edges with milk and pressing together. Brush the top with milk, then make a slit in the centre of the pie lid to let steam escape.

Bake for 30 minutes, or until golden brown, then sprinkle the caster sugar on top and serve.

CLASSIC CHOCOLATE MOUSSE

If avocado's not your thing (see page 9), try the classic version instead. Chocolate mousse never dates, and it's easy to see why. Light, fluffy and perfect served with berries.

———————— | *Serves 4–6* | ————————

Ingredients

125 g dark chocolate (ideally 70% minimum cocoa solids)

4 large eggs (separated)

1 ½ tbsp coffee or orange liqueur (optional)

3 tsp caster sugar

Preparation method

Melt the chocolate in a heatproof bowl over a pan of simmering water, making sure the bowl does not touch the water.

As soon as the chocolate is fully melted, remove from the heat, drop in the egg yolks and beat until the mixture begins to thicken.

Stir in the liqueur (if using) and allow to cool.

Whisk the egg whites until they form soft peaks, then whisk in the sugar.

Pour the chocolate mixture into the beaten egg whites and fold together.

Put the mousse into a large bowl, or divide between individual glasses or bowls, and refrigerate overnight.

Tip

You can also use brandy or amaretto in place of the liqueur.

PORTUGUESE CUSTARD TARTS

If finger food is what you fancy, look no further than these traditional Portuguese tarts. Crisp pastry filled with creamy, wobbly custard. What's not to like?

———————————————| *Serves 10–12* |———————————————

Ingredients

1 vanilla pod

120 g caster sugar

3 egg yolks

2 tbsp cornflour

400 ml milk (full-fat)

Butter for greasing

1 pack of ready-rolled puff pastry (300–320 g)

Cinnamon to sprinkle (optional)

Preparation method

Split the vanilla pod and scrape out the seeds. Set aside.

In a pan, over a low heat, whisk together the sugar, egg yolks and cornflour until the mixture begins to thicken.

Gradually pour in the milk, together with the vanilla seeds, continuing to whisk until everything is mixed together fully and beginning to thicken.

Continue to stir until the custard comes to the boil, then remove from the heat and cover the surface with either baking parchment or cling film to prevent a skin from forming.

Use the butter to grease a 12-hole muffin tin, and preheat the oven to 190°C.

Put the pastry sheet on a lightly floured surface and roll to form a thick sausage shape. Cut into 10–12 evenly sized slices, then roll out each one individually to around 9–10 cm in diameter.

Line each hole of the muffin tin with one of the pastry discs. Don't worry if the edges bunch up a bit – the rustic look is what you're after!

Divide the cooled custard between the pastry cases. Bake for around 20 minutes or until the pastry is golden and the custard set and browning on top.

Remove from the oven and allow the tarts to cool in the tin for 5–10 minutes before placing on a wire rack to cool further.

Best served warm or at room temperature, sprinkled with cinnamon if desired.

BAKEWELL TART

If legend is to be believed, Bakewell tart (not to be confused with Bakewell pudding) was the result of an error in the kitchen. Which just goes to show that some mistakes are worth making.

―――――――――――――― Serves 8 ――――――――――――――

Ingredients

For the pastry:

110 g butter
Pinch of salt
225 g plain flour
2 tsp caster sugar
1 egg yolk
1 tsp water

For the filling:

3 tbsp raspberry jam
  (more if you like!)
100 g butter
100 g caster sugar
2 eggs
100 g ground almonds
25 g plain flour
25 g flaked almonds
  to decorate

Preparation method

Dice the butter and put into a large bowl, before adding the salt and sifting in the flour. Rub together using your fingertips until the mixture resembles breadcrumbs.

Add the sugar and egg yolk. Mix, adding a splash of water if it's not binding fully, to form a dough. Wrap the dough in cling film and chill in the fridge for 30 minutes.

Preheat the oven to 190°C. Grease a 23-cm tart tin.

On a lightly floured work surface, gently roll out the pastry thin enough to line the tin, with excess pastry over the sides.

Line the pastry with baking paper, fill with baking beans and blind bake for 15 minutes. Remove the baking paper and beans, and return to the oven for a further 5 minutes, or until golden brown. Allow to cool then spread the base with an even layer of jam.

To make the frangipane filling, beat together the butter and sugar until fluffy. Add the eggs, one at a time, while beating continuously. Fold in the ground almonds and the flour.

Spread the mixture evenly over the jam and bake for 20 minutes. Sprinkle the flaked almonds on top and return to the oven for 5–10 minutes or until the sponge is golden brown. Allow the tart to cool in the tin.

"

JUST LIKE MOTHER
USED TO MAKE. A QUICK
POLL OF DESSERT LOVERS
SHOWS THAT THESE ARE
THE PREFERRED PUDS TO
HAND DOWN THROUGH
THE GENERATIONS.

"

FAMILY-
FAVOURITE
PUDDINGS

CHOCOLATE FUDGE PUDDING

Chocolate is well known as a feel-good food. But when it's hot, melting and gooey? It's a feel-VERY-good food indeed.

———— Serves 4 ————

Ingredients

For the sponge:

75 g self-raising flour
25 g cocoa powder
Pinch of salt
110 g muscovado sugar
110 g butter
1 tsp vanilla extract
2 eggs
2–3 tbsp milk

For the sauce:

75 g muscovado sugar
25 g cocoa powder
200 ml milk

Preparation method

Preheat the oven to 180°C. Grease a 1-litre ovenproof dish.

In a large bowl, sift the flour, and add the cocoa powder and salt.

In a separate bowl, beat the sugar, butter and vanilla extract together until light and fluffy. Beat the eggs and then add gradually to the mix. Pour this mixture into the first bowl, and fold to combine, adding just enough milk so that the mixture drops easily off the spoon.

For the sauce, mix the sugar and cocoa powder in a small bowl and add the milk, beating until smooth.

Transfer the sponge mixture into the ovenproof dish, then pour the sauce on top.

Bake for 45–60 minutes.

Best served with vanilla ice cream and fresh berries.

BLACKBERRY AND APPLE CRUMBLE

Rich purple, sugary fruit and crisp golden crumble. What better bowlful to curl up with on an autumnal evening?

———————————| *Serves 4* |———————————

Ingredients

For the filling:

3 cooking apples
25 g butter
150 g caster sugar
75 g fresh blackberries

For the crumble:

110 g plain flour
50 g butter
50 g caster sugar

Preparation method

Preheat the oven to 180°C.

Peel, core and slice the apples.

Dice the butter and gently heat in a small pan until melted, then add the apple slices and cook gently until they soften. Add the sugar, and stir well.

Once the sugar has melted, add the blackberries and stir, then remove from the heat.

In a large bowl, sift the flour, and add the butter and sugar. Use your fingertips to rub together to create a coarse, breadcrumb texture.

Transfer the filling into a 23-cm ovenproof dish. Sprinkle the crumble mixture on top of the filling, making sure you leave no gaps around the sides.

Bake for 20 minutes, or until golden brown.

QUEEN OF PUDDINGS

Trifle meets meringue in this warm, sticky dessert that's been a family favourite for decades.

———————————— Serves 6 ————————————

Ingredients

80 g fresh breadcrumbs
Grated rind of 1 lemon
1 tsp vanilla extract
90 g caster sugar
425 ml milk

25 g butter (plus extra for greasing)
3 eggs
3 tbsp raspberry jam

Preparation method

Preheat the oven to 170°C and grease a shallow 1.5-litre ovenproof dish.

Add the breadcrumbs, lemon zest, vanilla and 1 tbsp (15 g) caster sugar to the dish.

In a small saucepan, gently warm the milk and the butter until they reach a simmer.

Pour over the breadcrumb mix and stir to combine.

Leave to stand for 10–15 minutes, to allow the breadcrumbs to absorb the liquid.

Separate the eggs, beat the yolks and then add slowly to the crumb mix, mixing well.

Bake for 20–25 minutes or until the custard is firm.

Remove from the oven. While it cools, make the meringue by whisking the egg whites until they form stiff peaks.

Whisk in the remaining sugar, a tablespoon at a time, until the meringue is stiff and glossy.

Warm the jam until it melts and then spread evenly over the custard.

Top with the meringue (you can pipe it, if you prefer).

Return to the oven for 20 minutes or until the meringue turns light/golden brown.

Serve hot.

LEMON MERINGUE PIE

The classic mix of tart lemon and sweet, fluffy meringue makes this the perfect centrepiece for any occasion.

———————— ⊦ *Serves 6–8* ⊦ ————————

Ingredients

For the pastry:

110 g butter
Pinch of salt
225 g plain flour
2 tsp caster sugar
1 egg yolk
1 tsp water

For the lemon curd:

110 g caster sugar
7 tbsp cornflour
60 ml water
Grated zest and juice of
   4 lemons
6 egg yolks
110 g butter (melted)

For the meringue:

6 egg whites
300 g caster sugar

Preparation method

Dice the butter then place in a large bowl, add the salt and sift in the flour. Rub together using your fingertips until the mixture resembles breadcrumbs.

Add the sugar and egg yolk, and mix to form a dough. If it seems a little dry, you can add a splash of water.

Wrap the dough in cling film and chill in the fridge for 30 minutes.

Preheat the oven to 190°C. Grease a 23-cm tart tin.

On a lightly floured work surface, gently roll out the pastry thin enough to line the tin, with excess pastry over the sides.

Line the pastry with baking paper, fill with baking beans and blind bake for 15 minutes. Remove the baking paper and beans, and return to the oven for a further 5 minutes, or until golden brown.

Reduce the heat of the oven to 150°C. Tidy the edges of the pastry using a sharp knife.

In a large bowl, mix the sugar and cornflour with enough water so that it forms a paste.

Gently heat the rest of the water with the lemon zest in a small pan until it comes to the boil, then pour into the bowl and whisk to combine.

Beat in the lemon juice, egg yolks and butter. Pour back into the pan. Heat gently until the mixture thickens, then pour into the pastry case and leave to stand for 5 minutes.

In a large bowl, whisk the egg whites vigorously until they form stiff peaks, then gradually add the sugar, whisking all the time. Transfer the meringue onto the lemon curd, and bake for 40 minutes.

CHERRY CLAFOUTIS

Golden batter studded with juicy cherries… Few things say 'eat me' quite like this fruity French classic.

———————| *Serves 6* |———————

Ingredients

*30 g butter plus extra
  for greasing*
400 g cherries
3 eggs
75 g golden caster sugar

65 g plain flour
½ tsp baking powder
240 ml whole milk
1 tsp vanilla essence
Icing sugar for dusting

Preparation method

Preheat the oven to 180°C and grease a shallow ovenproof dish (around 23 cm). Stone the cherries then place in the dish.

Beat the eggs and sugar together until fluffy, then sieve in the flour, add the baking powder, milk and vanilla, and whisk together until you have a smooth batter.

Melt the butter and add to the batter before pouring over the cherries. Bake for 30–35 minutes or until risen and golden. Serve warm, dusted with icing sugar.

"

THERE'S NO PLACE FOR
STEAMING SPONGES OR
PIPING HOT PIES ON A
BOILING SUMMER'S DAY.
BUT DOES THAT MEAN YOU
SHOULD FORGO DESSERT
ALTOGETHER? HEAVENS NO!

"

SUMMER
PUDDINGS

NO-BAKE CHEESECAKE

A perennial favourite – plus you don't even need to switch the oven on. This definitely counts as a win-win.

———————— ⊣ *Serves 8* ⊢ ————————

Ingredients

150 g digestive biscuits
75 g butter
100 g icing sugar
1 tsp vanilla extract

500 g full fat cream cheese
200 ml double cream
Fruit to serve

Preparation method

Line a 20-cm tin with baking parchment. A spring-form tin is best but a loose-bottomed tin will be fine if you don't have one.

Crush the biscuits into fine crumbs.

Melt the butter and combine with the biscuit crumbs until thoroughly mixed.

Tip into the tin and press down firmly to form an even base.

Refrigerate for at least an hour or until set.

Beat together the icing sugar, vanilla essence and cream cheese until smooth.

Add the cream and continue mixing until fully combined. Spoon the mixture onto the base, pushing it down to ensure there are no air bubbles trapped inside.

Smooth the top and then chill until set. Ideally leave overnight – but if you don't have time, at least an hour.

To serve, top with the fruit of your choice. Strawberries or a pile of summer fruits work perfectly.

Tip

There are countless ways to vary this – why not try lemon and ginger? (Replace the digestives with ginger nuts and the vanilla with the zest and juice of one lemon. You can stir in some lemon curd for extra richness if desired.) The possibilities are endless!

CHILLED FRUIT SOUP

Refreshing, cool, and the simplest way to add a touch of sophistication and sparkle to any summer dinner party.

———————| *Serves 4* |———————

Ingredients

400 g strawberries
50 g caster sugar
1 bottle champagne or sparkling white wine
Mixed summer fruit to garnish

Preparation method

Puree the strawberries with the sugar and refrigerate until needed.

Just before serving, add champagne to desired consistency, stir and serve in soup bowls, garnished with summer fruits – blueberries, raspberries, redcurrants and sliced peaches work well.

FANCY FRUIT SALAD

Herbs with fruit sounds a bit strange, until you remember that basil pairs perfectly with strawberries, and mint works beautifully with melons, citrus and more. Sometimes simple is best.

———————————— Serves 4 ————————————

Ingredients

*700 g fruit, e.g.
  strawberries, raspberries
  and nectarines or peaches*

4 large mint leaves

4 large basil leaves

1 tbsp caster sugar

1 tbsp lime juice

Preparation method

Hull the strawberries and cut into halves or quarters depending on the size. Stone and dice the peaches or nectarines. Mix together with the raspberries.

Finely chop the herbs and combine with the sugar. Mix gently into the fruit (you don't want to break it up) with the lime juice and chill.

Serve garnished with a sprig of mint.

SUMMER FRUIT FOOL

Prove you're no fool by offering guests this delicious summer dessert.

———————| Serves 4–6 |———————

Ingredients

500 g summer fruit, e.g.
strawberries (hulled)
and raspberries

2 tbsp golden caster sugar

300 ml double cream
100 ml natural yogurt

Preparation method

Lightly mash the fruit and mix with the sugar (you can blend to a smoother puree if preferred).

Whip the cream in a bowl until it forms soft peaks.

Fold in the yogurt.

Fold in the fruit. You don't want it to look too uniform – streaks are good!

Divide between individual glasses or glass bowls and chill before serving.

ETON MESS

What is a traditional British summer lunch without a traditional British summer dessert? They come no finer than this.

———————————————| Serves 4 |———————————————

Ingredients

450 g soft fruit, e.g. strawberries or a mix of strawberries, raspberries, blueberries, etc.

300 ml whipping or double cream

100 g meringue

Preparation method

Rinse and hull the strawberries and chop into pieces.

Place the whipping or double cream in a large bowl and whip until light and fluffy. Do not over-whip.

Break the meringue into bite-sized chunks and gently stir into the cream along with the fruit, avoiding being too vigorous – the fruit should keep its shape. Chill in the fridge before spooning into glass bowls to serve.

LEMON SYLLABUB

Another quick, creamy dessert – this time with an alcoholic twist. Definitely one for the grown-ups!

———————————— Serves 4 ————————————

Ingredients

60 ml white wine

50 g caster sugar

Finely grated rind and juice of 1 lemon

200 ml double or whipping cream

Preparation method

Mix together the wine, sugar, lemon juice and half the rind. Leave to infuse, ideally overnight.

Whip the cream until it forms soft peaks.

Gently fold in the infused mixture from the fridge.

Divide between glasses or glass bowls and chill for at least an hour.

Sprinkle with the remaining rind to serve.

Tip

Like the fruit fool, syllabub works brilliantly with a biscuit (or two) on the side for dipping (it's definitely a dipping rather than a dunking kind of dessert!).

If you don't have time to infuse the wine and lemon mixture overnight, pop it in a pan and heat gently until the sugar is dissolved. Cool before folding into the whipped cream. It won't have quite the same intensity, but it will still taste delicious.

MANGO AND LIME SORBET

Easier than ice cream – and healthier too. What's not to love about this vibrant – and gloriously orange – iced dessert?

———————— Serves 6–8 ————————

Ingredients

3 large mangoes
250 g caster sugar
Juice of 2 limes
300 ml water

Preparation method

Peel and stone the mangoes and cut the flesh into chunks.

Put the sugar and lime juice into a small pan with the water. Heat gently until the sugar has dissolved.

Once the syrup has cooled, blend together with the mango flesh to form a smooth puree.

Pour the mixture into a shallow dish (make sure it's freezer-proof!) and pop in the freezer.

To prevent crystals forming, you will need to break up the mixture every 30 minutes or so. The best way to do this is to stir thoroughly with a fork before refreezing and repeating the process as needed until smooth (around four or five times over 2–3 hours).

Once it's reached the desired consistency, serve or transfer to a storage container, cover and freeze until needed. It will keep for at least a month.

Tip

Try using different fruits for equally delicious results – raspberries work particularly well.

SUMMER PUDDING

Easy but impressive – which is always a bonus. There's no better way to use up a glut of summer fruit.

———————————————| *Serves 6* |———————————————

Ingredients

1 kg summer fruit (strawberries, raspberries, blackberries, blackcurrants and redcurrants) plus a little extra to serve

150 g golden caster sugar

3 tbsp water

7–8 slices white bread

Preparation method

Put the fruit (except the strawberries), the sugar and the water into a large pan and heat very gently until the sugar dissolves.

Continue to cook for a couple of minutes, until the fruit begins to soften – stir occasionally but take care not to break up the fruit.

Mix in the strawberries – if these are large, cut them into halves/quarters – and remove from the heat.

Drain the fruit over a large bowl, reserving the deep red juice.

Line a 1.25-litre pudding basin with cling film – this makes it much easier to turn out the finished pudding. Leave an overhang big enough to cover the base of the pudding once it's assembled.

Remove the crusts from the bread, then cut a large square from one of the slices of bread, dip it into the juice (don't let it get sodden) and push it snugly (juice side down) into the base of the bowl. (Make sure it's big enough to cover the bottom of the bowl and leave an overlap).

Cut the rest of the bread slices in half lengthwise, repeat the dipping process, and use to line the sides of the bowl, pressing them in firmly. Overlap the slices slightly to ensure there are no gaps in the finished pudding.

Carefully spoon the fruit into the bread-lined bowl, pushing it down to ensure there are no gaps.

Seal the pudding using the remaining bread (dipping as before).

Use the cling film to cover the pudding and place a saucer or small plate on top. You will need to weigh this down in order to keep the fruit and bread in place – tin cans (full, of course) are great for this.

Refrigerate – ideally overnight – to allow the bread to absorb the juices.

If you have any fruit or juice left over you can use them to make a sauce.

Turn the pudding out carefully onto a serving plate and top with fresh berries or redcurrants.

Serve with double cream.

Tip

Bread that's a day or two old works better than fresh. Use medium or thick slices rather than thin.

EASY VANILLA ICE CREAM

The simplest of desserts, this easy-peasy ice cream doesn't need to be churned at all. Delicious on its own or with a handful of summer berries.

——————————————— Serves 6–8 ———————————————

Ingredients

½ 397-g can sweetened condensed milk

600 ml double cream

1 tsp vanilla extract

Preparation method

Place the condensed milk, cream and vanilla in a large bowl.

Use an electric whisk to beat the mixture until it's stiff and has the consistency of clotted cream.

Spatula into a freezer container or loaf tin, cover with cling film and freeze until firm.

"

WE WEREN'T SORRY TO
BID FAREWELL TO BELL
BOTTOMS, CHEESECLOTH
AND POLYESTER, BUT 70s
FASHION HAD ITS MOMENTS,
NOT LEAST ON THE DINNER
TABLE. THESE PUDS ARE TOO
GOOD TO EVER BE PASSÉ.

"

RETRO
PUDDINGS

BANANA SPLIT

Less a recipe, more an assembly job. This childhood favourite couldn't be easier to make.

———————————| Serves 4 |———————————

Ingredients

50 g dark chocolate (70% minimum cocoa solids)

50 g quality milk chocolate

250 ml double cream

4 bananas

Ice cream (according to preference, but vanilla and chocolate both work perfectly)

Whipped or squirty cream (optional)

Maraschino or glacé cherries to decorate (optional)

Chopped hazelnuts to serve (optional)

Preparation method

To make the chocolate sauce, chop the chocolate finely and put into a heatproof bowl.

In a small pan, heat the cream until it reaches boiling point and then pour over the chocolate pieces.

Allow the chocolate to melt (at this stage it doesn't look particularly appetising!) and then stir gently to combine into a rich, glossy sauce.

Split the bananas lengthwise and place both halves in a banana boat or other small oval dish.

Between the halves add three small scoops of ice cream – tradition dictates vanilla or a mix of vanilla, chocolate and strawberry.

Top each scoop with a swirl of cream and a cherry, then sprinkle with chopped nuts and serve immediately, drizzled with the chocolate sauce.

Tip

Why not experiment with different ice cream flavours and toppings? The best thing about this dessert is that anything goes!

PINEAPPLE UPSIDE-DOWN CAKE

Retro, yes. But some things are so good they stand the test of time. Leftovers taste just as good served cold – if indeed they last that long!

———————————| Serves 4 |———————————

Ingredients

1 can pineapple rings
50 g light muscovado or soft brown sugar
2 tbsp golden syrup
175 g butter or margarine
125 g caster sugar
125 g self-raising flour
2 eggs

Preparation method

Preheat the oven to 190°C.

Grease a 20-cm tin (don't use a loose-bottomed one or you will lose half the sauce).

Drain the pineapple and arrange it in a single layer over the base of the tin.

In a saucepan, melt the muscovado or brown sugar with the syrup and 50 g of the butter. Simmer until golden brown and smooth.

Pour over the pineapple.

Beat the rest of the butter with the sugar, flour and eggs to make the sponge. Spoon the mixture carefully on top of the pineapple and sauce.

Bake for around 35 minutes until golden brown and firm on top.

Allow to cool in the tin for 5–10 minutes before carefully turning out onto a large plate.

Serve with ice cream or cream.

APPLE FRITTERS

Apple blanketed in crisp golden batter – as pleasing to the eye as it is to the palate. (Which is very pleasing indeed.)

———————— Serves 4 ————————

Ingredients

100 g plain flour
1 tbsp caster sugar
Pinch of salt
1 egg
150 ml milk

2 apples
Lemon juice
Vegetable oil for frying
*Golden syrup and vanilla
    ice cream to serve*

Preparation method

Sift the flour and fold in the sugar and the salt.

Beat together the egg and the milk and add slowly to the dry ingredients, beating until it's smooth and the consistency of double cream. Pour into a shallow bowl.

Prepare the apples by peeling, coring and slicing into rings. Toss the pieces in a little lemon juice to prevent them from browning.

Heat the oil in a deep frying pan (a wok is ideal). To ensure it's the right temperature, try dropping a small cube of bread or a drop of batter into the pan – if it turns golden then it's hot enough.

In batches, coat the apple pieces in the batter and then fry until crisp and golden brown. Don't crowd the pan or the fritters will go soggy.

Drain the fritters on kitchen paper and serve hot, drizzled with golden syrup. Cold, creamy vanilla ice cream goes perfectly with the hot, crispy fruit.

Tip

This works really well with bananas or pineapple rings, too.

SIMPLE SHERRY TRIFLE

Luscious layers of jelly, custard and cream sitting on top of sweet, boozy sponge. A sure-fire winner for any occasion – or non-occasion!

———————————————— | Serves 8 | ————————————————

Ingredients

1 packet trifle sponges
4 tbsp sherry
1 tin of fruit cocktail
1 packet strawberry jelly
2 tbsp custard powder

1 tbsp caster sugar
570 ml milk
300 ml double cream
Toasted flaked almonds
  to decorate

Preparation method

Slice the sponges in half horizontally and lay over the base of a glass bowl. Pour the sherry over and allow to soak in.

Drain the fruit cocktail and arrange on top of the sponge. Make up the jelly according to the packet instructions and pour over the fruit. Refrigerate until set.

To make the custard, put the powder and sugar into a bowl and use a couple of tablespoons of the milk to mix into a smooth paste.

In a small pan, heat the rest of the milk to a simmer and then add to the custard and sugar mix.

Stir well before returning to the pan and heating gently until it comes to the boil, while stirring continuously to avoid lumps.

Remove from the heat and leave to cool – cover the surface with cling film or baking parchment to prevent a skin forming.

Spoon the cooled custard onto the set jelly to form an even layer. Return to the fridge while you whip the cream until it forms soft peaks.

Carefully spoon or pipe the cream over the custard, scatter the almonds on top and refrigerate until serving.

For a retro look, replace the flaked almonds with sprinkles, hundreds and thousands and/or silver balls.

CARAMELISED ORANGES

There's a touch of the seventies about this simple dessert, which, fortunately, can be enjoyed even in the absence of flares or a hostess trolley.

—————————————| Serves 4 |—————————————

Ingredients

4 oranges
175 g caster sugar
175 ml water

Preparation method

Peel the oranges and remove any pith. Slice into thin rounds (6 or 7 per orange, depending on the size), removing any pips.

Put the sugar and half the water into a pan and heat until the sugar dissolves, stirring regularly.

Bring to the boil and simmer gently until the syrup turns golden brown.

Remove pan from the heat and add the remaining water. Note that the syrup will be extremely hot and that the addition of water will make it bubble and spit. It's a good idea to keep as far back as possible and use an oven glove.

Stir to remove any lumps. If any prove particularly stubborn return the pan to a low heat until they have melted.

Pour the syrup over the orange segments and leave to cool before serving.

CHOCOLATE FONDUE

Dipping bread into molten cheese is one thing. Dipping fruit into rich molten chocolate is another altogether.

———————— ⊢ *Serves 4* ⊣ ————————

Ingredients

200 g dark chocolate, ideally 70% minimum cocoa solids

300 ml pot double cream

40 g butter

1 tbsp brandy (optional)

500 g fruit – whole strawberries (hulled), grapes, and chunks of pineapple and banana

Marshmallows (optional)

Preparation method

Break the chocolate into small pieces and put it, with the cream and butter, into a small pan, heating gently until the chocolate melts. Remove from the heat. This may look like it's never going to come together to make a smooth sauce, but judicious stirring will allow the ingredients to combine. Add the brandy last, if desired.

If you have a fondue set, pour the sauce into the pot and keep warm with the flame beneath – it may need the odd stir.

If you don't have a set, pour from pan to serving dish and serve immediately!

Pile the fruit onto a platter and hand each guest a skewer for spearing and dipping. Warning – this can get messy! But it's worth it.

"

IMPRESS YOUR GUESTS WITH
THESE DELICIOUS DESSERTS
THAT ALLOW YOU TO SPEND
TIME AT THE TABLE AND
NOT RACING ROUND THE
KITCHEN IN A PANIC.

"

DINNER–
PARTY
PUDDINGS

CHOCOLATE BROWNIE TORTE

A rich chocolate dessert is a sure way to have your guests eating out of your hand. Not literally, of course – I've found using plates creates far less mess!

⊢ *Serves 8* ⊢

Ingredients

4 eggs

225 g caster sugar

2 drops of vanilla essence

150 g dark chocolate (use 70% minimum cocoa solids)

125 g unsalted butter

50 ml water

25 g plain flour

50 g ground almonds

Preparation method

Preheat oven to 180°C.

Grease and line an 18-cm spring-form cake tin.

Break the eggs into a bowl and whisk together with the sugar and vanilla essence until light and fluffy.

Meanwhile, put the chocolate, butter and water into a heatproof bowl, then place over a pan of simmering water, making sure the bowl does not touch the water.

Once melted, gently stir all ingredients together.

Using a metal spoon gently fold the creamed eggs-and-sugar mixture into the chocolate mix then stir in the flour and almonds.

Pour ingredients into a cake tin and bake for 30–40 minutes until the centre of the torte is still soft but a thin crust has formed on the surface.

Remove from oven and leave to cool.

PAVLOVA

Fluffy pillows of meringue topped with clouds of whipped cream and studded with fruit. A pud so good it really will make you want to dance.

—————————— *Serves 8* ——————————

Ingredients

4 large egg whites
2 level tsp cornflour
225 g caster sugar
1 tsp white wine vinegar
1 tsp vanilla essence
400 ml double or whipping cream

400 g summer fruits (a mix of strawberries, raspberries, blackberries, blueberries, etc.)
Icing sugar and sprigs of mint to garnish

Preparation method

Preheat the oven to 150°C.

Cover a large baking tray with baking parchment and mark out a template for your meringue (the easiest way to do this is to draw around a large dinner plate).

Whisk the egg whites until they form stiff peaks.

Mix together the cornflour and the sugar and add to the egg whites, a tablespoon at a time, whisking until combined.

Whisk in the vinegar and vanilla essence.

Pile the meringue into the circle, smoothing it out but ensuring that the edges are slightly higher than the centre.

Bake for an hour then turn off the oven and leave for another 30 minutes before removing and cooling completely.

Whip the cream until thick and spread over the meringue (leaving a couple of centimetres of meringue around the outside).

Top with the fruit (if using strawberries, hull and halve or quarter them depending on the size). Dust with icing sugar and top with a couple of sprigs of mint.

Tip

Vary this recipe by turning it into a tropical-fruit pavlova, replacing the berries with mango and passionfruit, and garnishing with toasted coconut.

TARTE TATIN

Fruit, caramel and buttery pastry... this famous French dessert tastes every bit as good as it looks. Works a treat with quality vanilla ice cream.

 Serves 6

Ingredients

375 g block of puff pastry*
100 g butter
150 g sugar (golden caster or soft light brown)
6 medium apples (Cox or Braeburn are best)

*Frozen pastry is fine but make sure it's fully defrosted before use. Try to find an all-butter pastry – it makes all the difference.

Preparation method

Preheat the oven to 180°C. You will need a 20-cm frying pan or round, shallow dish that can be used in the oven as well as on the stove top. If using a frying pan, make sure it has a metal handle – a plastic one will melt in the oven!

Peel, core and quarter the apples.

Put your pan/dish on the stove and heat the butter and the sugar until it bubbles, and then stir until the sugar caramelises and you are left with a rich brown liquid toffee – don't let it burn!

Arrange the apples on top (remember, the caramel will be extremely hot) and turn down the heat, cooking gently for around 5–10 minutes until the apples have started to soften and caramelise.

Roll out your pastry to around ½ cm in thickness, making sure it's bigger than your pan/dish by about 4 cm.

Lay it on top of the apples, then tuck the edges firmly down inside the edges of the pan – note that, at this stage, the caramel will still be very hot.

Prick a couple of holes in the top – this will allow steam to escape and stop the pastry going soggy.

Bake for 30–35 minutes or until the pastry is crisp and golden. Don't worry if some of the caramel bubbles up round the sides.

Allow it to cool in the dish for 30–40 minutes before carefully turning out onto a large plate. Serve warm or at room temperature.

PEARS BELLE HELENE

Say *bonsoir* to *poires belle Hélène* (to give it its correct title), otherwise known as poached pears with ice cream and chocolate sauce, which is a little less poetic. This is as easy as it is elegant and a perfect way to finish off a dinner party.

─────────────┤ *Serves 6* ├─────────────

Ingredients

200 ml cold water

200 g caster sugar

1 vanilla pod split in half (optional)

6 dessert pears (squat rather than long and skinny works best in terms of presentation)

300 g dark chocolate (ideally 70% minimum cocoa solids)

150 ml double cream

Good-quality vanilla ice cream to serve

Preparation method

First make a syrup by putting the water into a saucepan with the sugar and the vanilla pod if using.

Simmer, stirring occasionally, until the sugar has dissolved.

Peel the pears, ideally keeping the stalk attached, and place carefully into the syrup, making sure that they are fully submerged.

Simmer gently for 20–25 minutes until tender but not soggy, then remove the pan from the heat, leaving the fruit in the liquid for as long as you can (ideally overnight at least).

Make the chocolate sauce according to the recipe on page 68.

Remove the pears from their syrup and stand on individual plates (or in large bowls) with a scoop of vanilla ice cream.

Drizzle generously with the chocolate sauce and serve immediately.

Tip

Cut a little slice off the bottom of each pear before cooking – this will help it to stand upright.

For a finishing touch, toast some flaked almonds and scatter over the dessert before serving.

TIRAMISU

Like chocolate mousse (see page 32), this Italian classic never seems to date. For a special touch, try layering it in individual cocktail glasses – perfect dinner-party fare.

———————————| Serves 4–6 |———————————

Ingredients

3 eggs
1½ tbsp sugar
250 g mascarpone
2 tbsp brandy

175 ml cold, strong coffee (espresso is ideal)
15–20 sponge finger (boudoir/ladyfinger) biscuits
2 tbsp cocoa powder

Preparation method

Separate the eggs.

Beat together the yolks and the sugar until fluffy.

Beat in the mascarpone and half the brandy.

Whisk the egg whites until they form stiff peaks, then fold into the mascarpone mixture.

Mix together the coffee and remaining brandy and pour into a shallow dish.

One by one, dip the biscuits (full length) into the coffee mixture and use half of them to line the bottom of the serving bowl (a glass bowl works best as it shows the layers).

Top with half the mascarpone mixture, sprinkle with half the cocoa powder then repeat the layers.

Dust the top with cocoa and refrigerate for 3–4 hours before serving.

Tip

Try grating chocolate on top in place of the remaining cocoa. You can also substitute the brandy with amaretto, rum or Marsala.

PANNA COTTA

Panna cotta – literally 'cooked cream' – is the perfect make-in-advance pud, and will delight diners with its elegant but distinctive wobble.

———————————— Serves 4 ————————————

Ingredients

2 leaves of gelatine
1 vanilla pod
250 ml double cream

250 ml whole milk
75 g caster sugar
Mint sprigs to decorate

Preparation method

Soak the gelatine leaves in cold water.

Split the vanilla pod and scrape out the seeds before setting them aside.

Put the rest of the ingredients into a pan – you can include just the vanilla seeds or leave the pod in to infuse the cream while it cooks.

Stir over a low heat until the sugar is dissolved, then bring to a simmer.

If using the vanilla pod, remove and discard at this stage. Remove from the heat and squeeze any excess water from the gelatine before mixing through the cream until it has fully dissolved.

Pour into four small moulds, ramekins or cups and chill until set.

If using moulds, turn out onto plates to serve – this way you get the full wobbly glory of the dessert. If you don't have suitable moulds, you can serve in cups or ramekins instead.

Tip

Sharp-tasting fruit is the perfect accompaniment to the sweet, mellow creaminess of the panna cotta. Raspberries, passion fruit or a berry compote all work really well.

POSH JELLY

Take an old favourite and turn it into something special:
this stunning dessert is fat-free too. Serve in clear glasses
for the full effect.

———————————————┤ Serves 6 ├———————————————

Ingredients

5 leaves of gelatine

50 g caster sugar

500 ml Prosecco or
champagne

150 g raspberries
(or a mix of raspberries,
blueberries and chopped
strawberries)

Preparation method

Soak the gelatine leaves in 75 ml cold water until they
soften (about 10 minutes). Put the sugar and 100 ml of
the champagne/Prosecco into a pan and heat gently
until all the sugar is dissolved. Remove from the heat.

Squeeze any excess water from the gelatine then add to
the pan, stirring well until fully combined. Stir in the rest
of the wine.

Divide the fruit between 6 glasses and pour the jelly mix
over. Refrigerate until set – ideally overnight.

FROZEN BERRIES WITH HOT CHOCOLATE SAUCE

This dish started life in one of London's top restaurants and has since found its way onto menus in eateries across the country – so it's clearly doing something right. Oh, and the hot/cold, sweet/sour combination is unbeatable.

 Serves 4

Ingredients

200 g good-quality white chocolate
200 ml double cream
500 g frozen berries

Preparation method

Break up the chocolate and put it, together with the cream, into a heatproof bowl over a pan of simmering water. Stir occasionally until the chocolate is fully melted.

Divide the berries between individual dishes, pour over the sauce and serve immediately.

If you're interested in finding out more
about our books, find us on Facebook
at **Summersdale Publishers** and follow
us on Twitter at **@Summersdale**.

Thanks very much for buying
this Summersdale book.

www.summersdale.com